The Life of

Florence Nightingale

Emma Lynch

Heinemann

www.heinemann.co.uk/library
Visit our website to find out more information about **Heinemann Library** books.

To order:
 Phone 44 (0) 1865 888066
 Send a fax to 44 (0) 1865 314091
 Visit the Heinemann Bookshop at www.heinemann.co.uk/library to browse our catalogue and order online.

First published in Great Britain by Heinemann Library, Halley Court, Jordan Hill, Oxford OX2 8EJ, part of Harcourt Education.
Heinemann is a registered trademark of Harcourt Education Ltd.

Editorial: Lucy Thunder and Harriet Milles
Design: Richard Parker and
    Tinstar Design Ltd (www.tinstar.co.uk)
Picture Research: Melissa Allison and Fiona Orbell
Production: Camilla Smith

Originated by Repro Multi-Warna
Printed and bound in China by
    South China Printing Company
The paper used to print this book comes from sustainable resources.

ISBN 0 431 18093 8
09 08 07 06 05
10 9 8 7 6 5 4 3 2 1

ISBN 0431 18185 3
10 09 08 07 06
10 9 8 7 6 5 4 3 2 1

British Library Cataloguing in Publication Data
Emma Lynch
Florence Nightingale. – (The Life of)
610.7'3'092
A full catalogue record for this book is available from the British Library.

Acknowledgements
The Publishers would like to thank the following for permission to reproduce photographs:
pp. **4**, **6**, **7**, **19**, **20**, **21**, **23**, **24**, **26**, **27** The Florence Nightingale Museum Trust; pp. **5**, **12**, **16** Mary Evans Picture Library; pp. **8**, **10** Hulton Archive/Getty Images; p. **9** National Portrait Gallery; pp. **11**, **13**, **15**, **18** The Wellcome Trust Medical Photograhic Library; p. **14** London Stills; p. **17** P&O Art Collection; p. **22** The National Army Museum; p. **25** Guy Stubbs/Corbis/ Gallo Images.

Cover photograph of Florence Nightingale, reproduced with permission of The Wellcome Trust Medical Photographic Library. Page icons: Hemera PhotoObjects.

The Publishers would like to thank Rebecca Vickers for her assistance in the preparation of this book.

Every effort has been made to contact copyright holders of any material reproduced in this book. Any omissions will be rectified in subsequent printings if notice is given to the Publishers.

Contents

Words shown in the text in bold, **like this**, are explained in the Glossary.

Who was Florence Nightingale?

Florence Nightingale was a famous nurse. She lived in the 1800s. People did not think nursing was an important job then. Florence made it very important.

This is Florence when she was 36 years old.

Florence looked after soldiers who were hurt in a war. She started the first nursing school in Britain. She also wrote a book that told nurses how to look after people.

This painting shows Florence visiting soldiers in hospital.

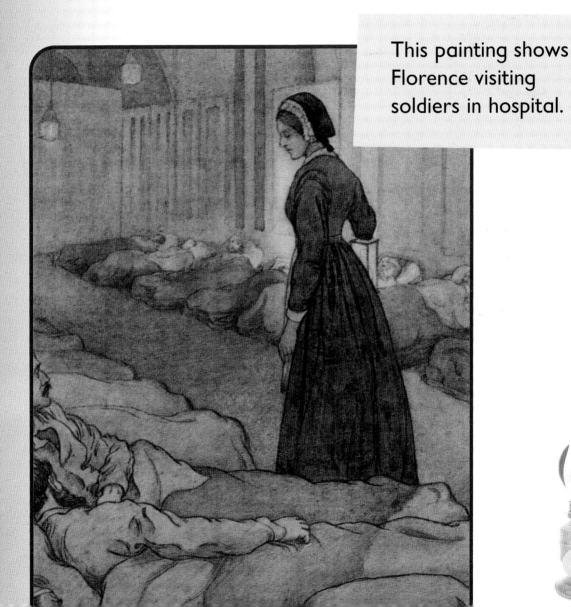

A happy childhood

Florence Nightingale was born on 12 May 1820. Her parents were visiting Italy. She was called Florence because she was born in a city in Italy called Florence.

This is Florence's father, William Nightingale. Florence's older sister, Parthenope, is sitting down.

In 1825, Florence's family moved to this house in Hampshire called Embley Park.

The family came back to live in England in 1821. Florence and her sister Parthenope had lessons at home. Florence was very good at maths.

Planning her future

Florence grew up into a young woman. Her parents wanted her to get married. They did not want her to have a job. Rich women did not work then.

This is a painting of Florence and Parthenope when they were young women.

On 7 February 1837, Florence felt that she heard God's voice asking her to work for him. She decided not to get married. She wanted to work for God.

When Richard Monckton Milnes asked Florence to marry him, she said no.

Caring for others

In the 1800s, many people died from diseases like **cholera**. Florence wanted to help sick people. She became sure that God wanted her to be a nurse.

When Florence was young, sick people were not well cared for.

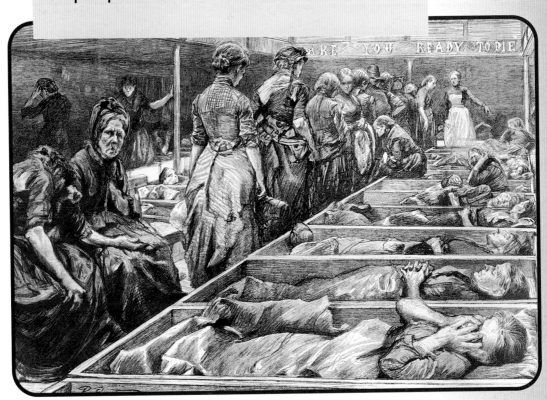

Florence heard about a special hospital in Germany. It had trained nurses. Nurses in England were not trained at that time. Nursing was not a **respectable** job.

This old cartoon makes fun of nurses.

Florence becomes a nurse

Florence's parents did not want her to be a nurse. They tried to stop her many times. This upset her so much that she became ill. Her parents sent her on holiday.

Florence visited beautiful places, like this, when she was on holiday.

In 1850, Florence went to visit the special hospital in Germany. When her parents found out, they punished her – even though she was 30 years old!

In 1851, Florence was allowed to train at the **Institution** of **Deaconesses** at Kaiserwerth in Germany.

Starting work

When Florence came home, a friend found her a job. She would run a small hospital. Florence's father was still angry, but he agreed to give her some money to live on.

The hospital was on Harley Street in London.

FLORENCE NIGHTINGALE LEFT HER HOSPITAL ON THIS SITE FOR THE CRIMEA • OCTOBER 21ST 1854

Florence started work on 12 August 1853. She had many new ideas for the hospital. Her biggest problem was that there were no trained nurses to help her.

Hospitals looked like this when Florence was a nurse.

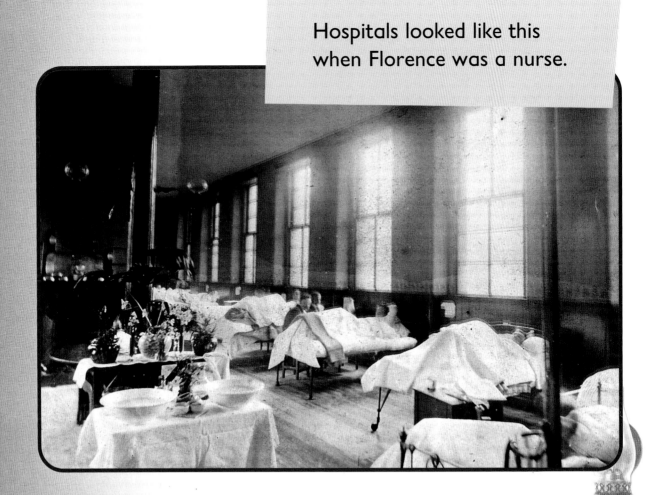

The Crimean War

In 1854, British soldiers went to fight in the **Crimean War**. Soldiers that were hurt were taken to army hospitals at Scutari, in Turkey.

The man in charge of the army was called Sidney Herbert.

Florence and her nurses sailed to Turkey on this ship. It was called *The Vectis*.

Sidney Herbert asked Florence to find nurses to go and help the soldiers. Florence left London on 21 October 1854. She went to Scutari with 38 other nurses.

The hospital at Scutari

Florence arrived at the hospital on 5 November 1854. It was a terrible place. There were rats everywhere. The toilets were just dirty holes in the ground.

The hospital at Scutari was called the Barrack Hospital.

There was no **furniture,** and nothing to cook with. Florence made sure that the hospital was cleaned. She **organized** work and **supplies**.

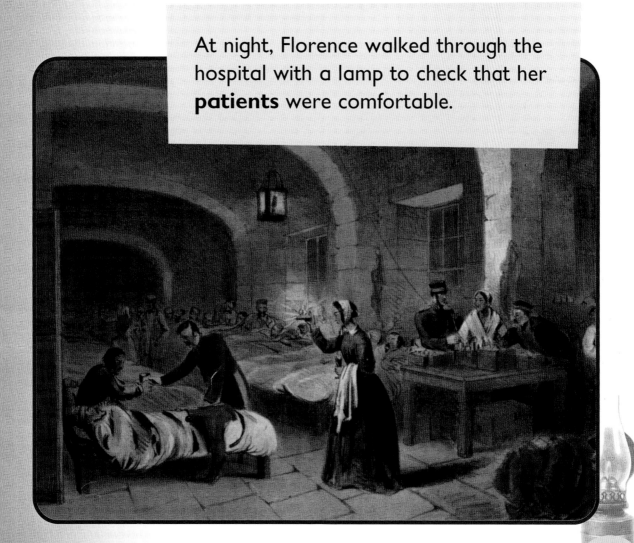

At night, Florence walked through the hospital with a lamp to check that her **patients** were comfortable.

Florence is a heroine!

Florence came back to Britain in 1856. She was a **heroine**. She met Queen Victoria in October 1856. Florence wrote an important report about what she had seen in the war.

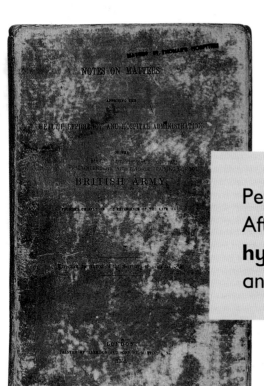

People read Florence's report. After that they made **hygiene** better in the army and in hospitals.

On 24 June 1860, Florence opened the Nightingale Training School for nurses. It was at St Thomas' Hospital in London. She had made nursing a **respectable** job.

Florence gave these gifts to the nurses at her school.

The end of a good life

Florence looked after other people all her life. She became ill herself, and went blind in 1901. Florence was given many **awards** for her work.

Florence was the first woman to be given the **Order of Merit**. She received it in 1907.

This is Florence when she was older.

Florence died on 13 August 1910, when she was 90 years old. A service was held at St Paul's Cathedral in London. People wanted to remember her life.

Why is Florence famous?

Florence believed that nurses should be trained to check their **patients**. They should make sure that patients are always kept clean and comfortable.

Florence is sitting with the nurses at the Nightingale Training School.

Florence also helped to make **hygiene** better. She knew that hospitals should be kept clean to stop **germs** spreading. She made life better for people in army hospitals.

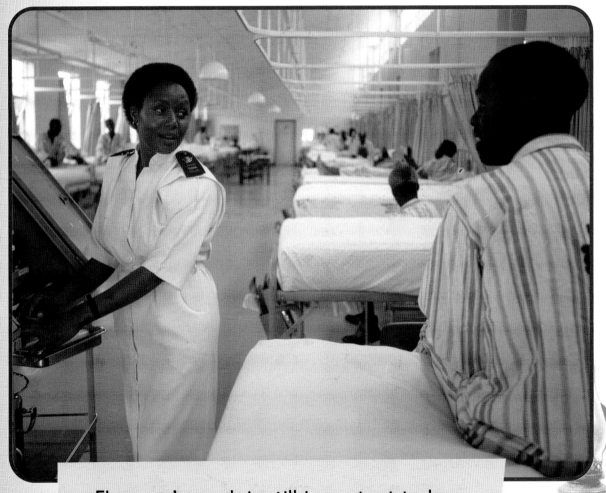

Florence's work is still important today.

More about Florence

There are many ways to find out about Florence. There are books, websites and **museums** about her life and work. We can also hear a sound recording of her voice.

We can still see Florence's lamp in a museum today.

We can find out more from Florence's own writing. She wrote letters, reports and books, and kept a diary. She even wrote notes all through her childhood.

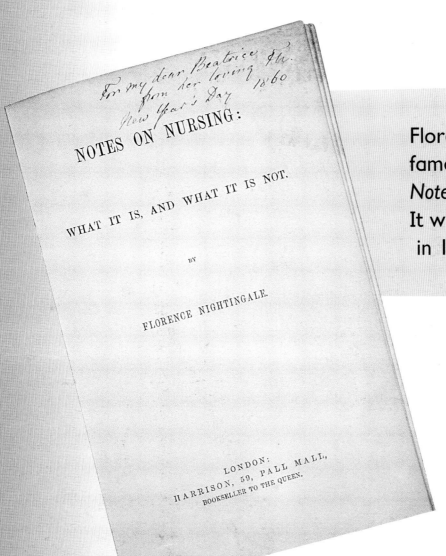

Florence's most famous book was *Notes on Nursing*. It was printed in 1859.

Fact file

- When Florence was a young woman, several men asked her to marry them. One of them was Richard Monckton Milnes. She would not marry him, but she always stayed friends with him.

- During the **Crimean War,** Florence walked around the hospital every night. She always carried a lamp. She wanted to see that her **patients** were comfortable. Because of this, she was called 'the lady with the lamp'.

- Some nurses and churches celebrate Florence Nightingale's life on or around 12 May every year. They would like this to become Florence Nightingale Day.

Timeline

1820   Florence is born in Florence, Italy on 12 May

1837   Florence thinks she hears God talking to her

1842   Florence finds out about the special hospital at Kaiserwerth in Germany

1851   Florence trains for three months in Kaiserwerth

1854   Florence travels to Scutari in Turkey. She cares for soldiers hurt in the **Crimean War**.

1856   Florence comes back to Britain

1860   The Nightingale Training School for nurses opens at St Thomas' Hospital, London

1907   Florence is the first woman to receive the **Order of Merit**

1910   Florence dies on 13 August

Glossary

award prize for doing something good

cholera disease that people catch from bad food or dirty water

Crimean War war fought by Britain and France against Russia between 1853 and 1856. Britain and France won the war.

deaconesses women who work for churches

furniture things for the home, such as beds, chairs and tables

germ something that can make you ill

heroine woman who is brave or good

hygiene keeping things clean and healthy

institution place where people go to learn

museum where pieces of art or parts of history are kept

Order of Merit prize given by the Queen

organize plan to make something happen

patient someone who is looked after by a doctor or nurse

respectable good, well behaved and honest

supplies things that people need, such as food or medicine

Find out more

Books

Famous People, Famous Lives: Florence Nightingale, Emma Fischel and Peter Kent (Franklin Watts, 2001)

How do we know about ...? Florence Nightingale and the Crimean War, Jane Shuter (Heinemann Library, 2004)

Websites

www.florence-nightingale.co.uk
A museum website about the famous nurse.

www.florence-nightingale-foundation.org.uk/
A website about Florence Nightingale and nursing.

Places to visit

Florence Nightingale Museum
St Thomas' Hospital
2 Lambeth Palace Road
London
SE1 7EW
Tel: 020 7620 0374

Index